An Adventure to the LIGHTHOUSE ISLAND

Answers to Children's Queries

Series - *Children's Knowledge Quest*

Author

M Borhan

From

Big 6 Publishing

This is the story of Allen, and his Adventure to the 'Lighthouse Island'; which is just few miles away from his house....where a stunning view of the island is directly seen from his home!
LightHouse Island
Allen's House

Yes, I have been there and with a lot of adventures and quest! Do you want to hear? Let me tell you...
Papa, what's that island with a Lighthouse? Did you go there?
Allen
Allen's Daughter

Many Years ago ....
From Breakfast to Afternoon, the Lighthouse had been in front of Allen all along from youth, giving him a source of imagination and all kinds of fascination...

Morning Sun
While Allen was an adult, the lighthouse had been a source of amazement for him all the time...From Music to Lyrics, he found there all he needed!

Meal Time
During Lunch or Dinner, the family members talked about the Lighthouse Island and its amazing history and the facts that always attracted many minds, not only from the past, but to present time till now!

Backward Balcony

When Allen Often got back home from Office, during afternoon, he enjoyed the scenic beauty even from the Backward Balcony of his home and the refreshing atmosphere with pure air at the balcony, which always gave him an aesthetic view....

One day, while in the front most balcony, Allen was thinking of doing something different....

The Lighthouse

Although, the Lighthouse seemed quite near from his seashore house, it's not possible just to swim or walk there! First, he needed to go to City Airport to the Island's Nearest Airport !

Front Corridor Balcony

Evening Time
He did just as he thought on that night! He booked a ticket for an Airline's Flight to the Lighthouse's nearest Port....

Airplane Window
Finally Fly
With a robust preparation, finally he boarded the 6-hour Island's Airplane Flight, hoping that soon he would land at the island's nearest airport!

Although, the lighthouse island was seen near, it had a complex path to reach...
Landing on Nearby Port
...and after landing on the nearest Island Airport, Allen decides to sail with a boat to the Lighthouse Island for the next paths...

After
taking the
Boat Journey...
Then the 2 hours boat journey from the Nearest
Port finishes and Allen now has finally reached
the Lighthouse Island !

Lighthouse Authority Office
&
Allen seems quite tired...
After a total of 8 hours hectic journey to the Island, Allen now has to face the Lighthouse Authority ...he has been told that he needed to understand the Rules & Regulations and sign Special Agreement Papers before he could go inside and climb the historic Lighthouse!

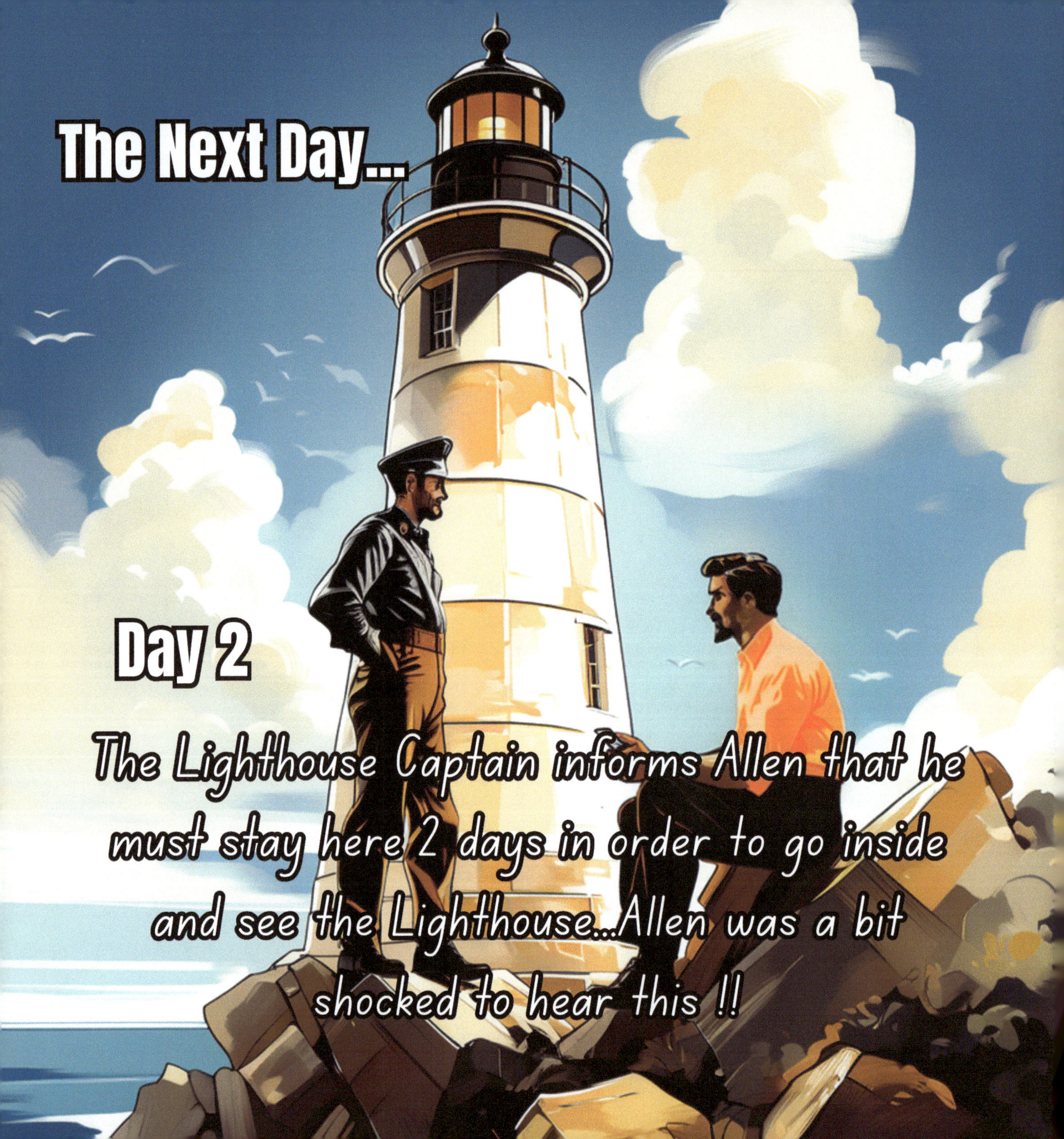

The Next Day...
Day 2
The Lighthouse Captain informs Allen that he must stay here 2 days in order to go inside and see the Lighthouse...Allen was a bit shocked to hear this !!

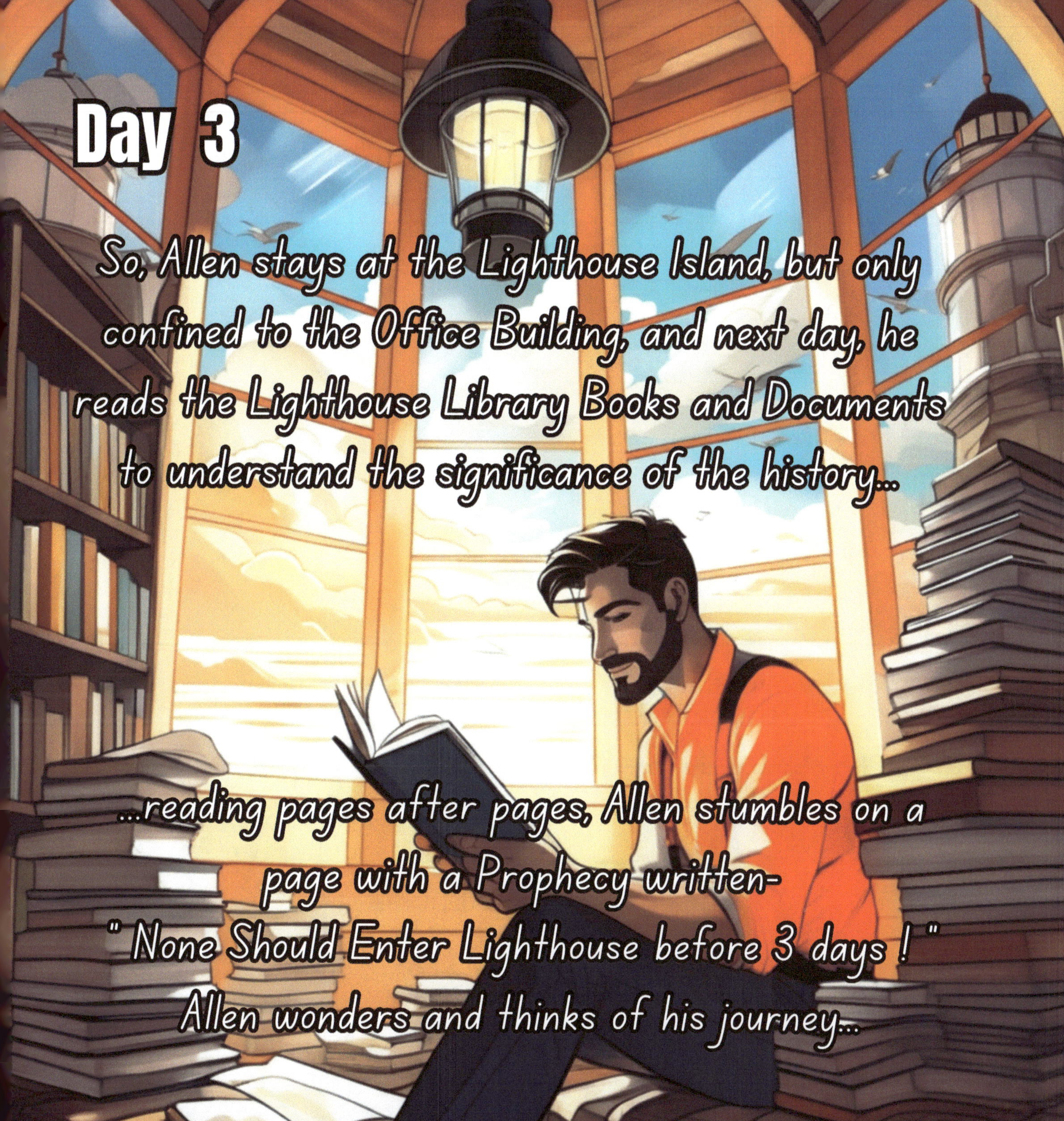

Day 3
So, Allen stays at the Lighthouse Island, but only confined to the Office Building, and next day, he reads the Lighthouse Library Books and Documents to understand the significance of the history...
...reading pages after pages, Allen stumbles on a page with a Prophecy written-
" None Should Enter Lighthouse before 3 days ! "
Allen wonders and thinks of his journey...

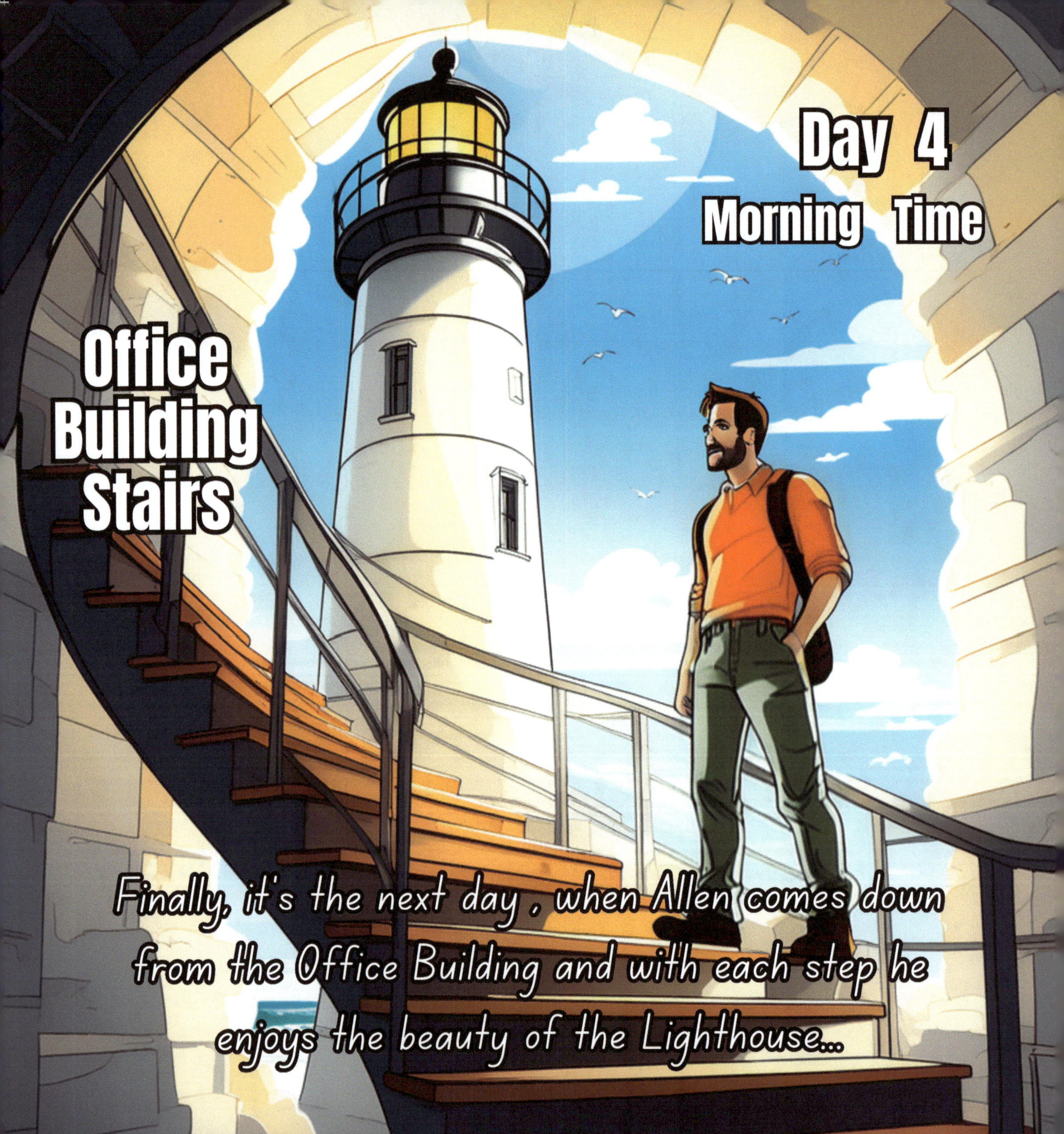
Day 4
Morning Time
Office
Building
Stairs
Finally, it's the next day , when Allen comes down
from the Office Building and with each step he
enjoys the beauty of the Lighthouse...

Office
Downstairs
Day 4
At Noon
Allen is few meters away from the Lighthouse, enjoying his last moments of just steps away from climbing the Lighthouse

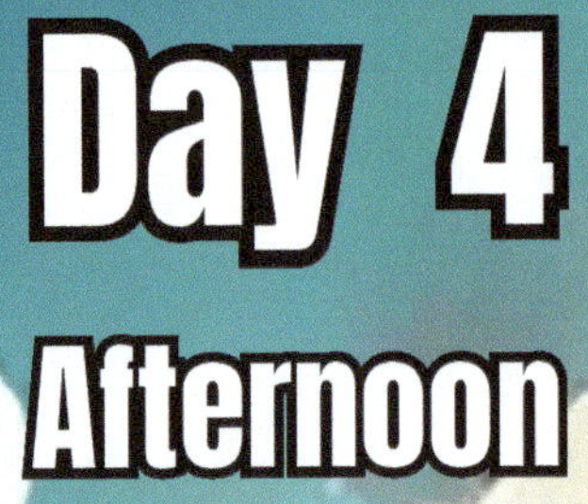

Day 4
Afternoon
After Hours of Waiting,
Allen gets final permission
from Office to go inside
the Lighthouse...now just
waiting to climb and
conquer the height...
The Lighthouse

Finally...
Allen at the bottom of Lighthouse on Front Gate, before climbing the Lighthouse

Top Floor
of
Lighthouse
Allen reaches the top most floor of the Lighthouse-
this is from where the furthest most broad horizons
can be seen...This is the moment he wanted to
conquer!

Evening Flight

Finally, Allen's journey finishes and he has enjoyed his quest to reach the Lighthouse...

Thus, Allen decides to take the Flight to home in the evening...

Reaching home, Allen sits to write all the history he read at the Library, Whatever he had seen inside the Lighthouse and experienced throughout this journey ...
Writing the Prophecy on Top -
" None Should Enter Lighthouse before 3 days! "

Grab Other Exciting Books

Book Series: Children's Nature Quest

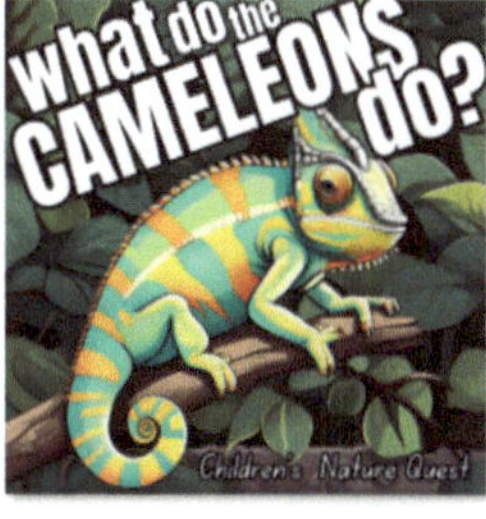

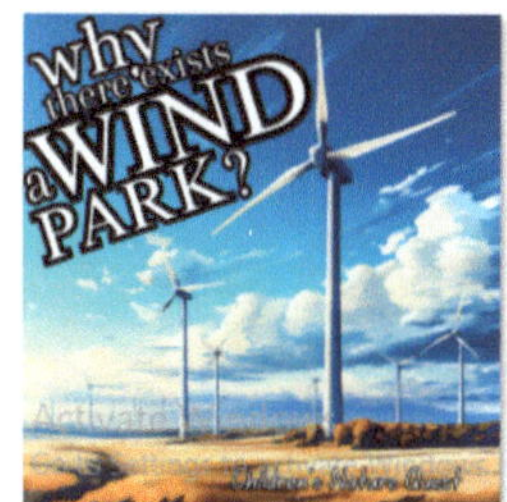

Book Series: Grizzly Bear Series

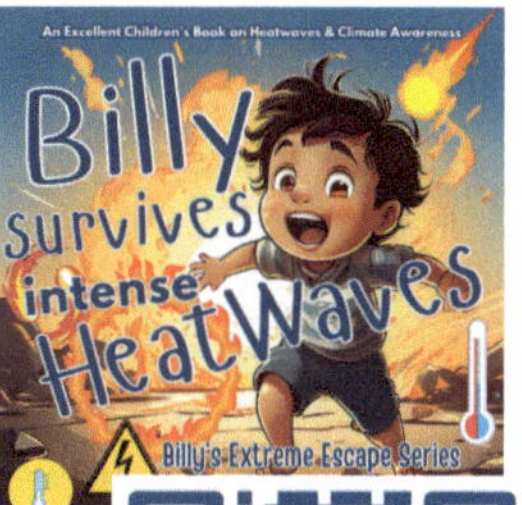

Other Series: Mixed Categories

Scan QRs, Follow & Like us

Instagram

Pinterest

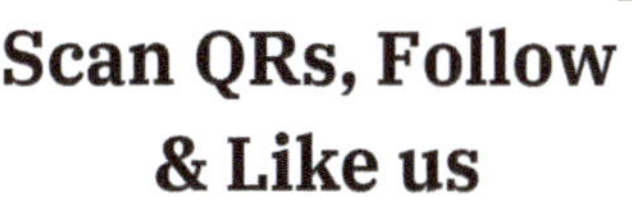

Tiktok